WE HELP YOUR BUSINESS GROW

Introduction

In today's competitive business landscape, growth isn't just a goal; it's a necessity. Whether you are a budding entrepreneur or a seasoned business owner, the ability to expand and evolve your business is crucial for long-term success. This book, "We Help Your Business Grow," is designed to provide you with actionable strategies, practical advice, and real-world case studies to help you navigate the complex journey of business growth.

In the ever-evolving landscape of modern business, achieving sustained growth can be a daunting challenge. Whether you're an entrepreneur starting from scratch or an established business looking to scale, "We

Help Your Business Grow" offers invaluable insights and practical strategies to elevate your enterprise to new heights.

THIS BOOK IS DESIGNED TO BE YOUR ROADMAP TO SUCCESS, PROVIDING YOU WITH:

1. **Proven Growth Strategies:** Discover time-tested methods and innovative approaches to expand your market reach, increase sales, and boost profitability.
2. **Digital Marketing Mastery:** Learn the latest digital marketing techniques, from social media strategies to SEO and content marketing, to effectively promote your brand and attract more customers.

3. **Financial Management:** Understand the fundamentals of financial planning, budgeting, and investment to ensure your business remains financially healthy and capable of sustained growth.

4. **Leadership and Team Building:** Explore effective leadership styles and team-building techniques that foster a productive, motivated workforce dedicated to achieving your business goals.

5. **Customer Relationship Management:** Gain insights into building strong, lasting relationships with your customers, enhancing customer satisfaction and loyalty.

6. **Innovation and Adaptability:** Embrace innovation and adaptability as key drivers of business growth, ensuring your enterprise stays ahead of the competition in an ever-changing market.

Throughout this book, you will find real-world case studies, expert advice, and actionable tips that you can implement immediately. Whether you are looking to refine your current business practices or embark on a new venture, "We Help Your Business Grow" is your essential guide to navigating the complexities of business growth and achieving long-term success.

Embark on this journey with us and transform your business into a thriving powerhouse.

TABLE OF CONTENT

1. **Introduction**
    a. Importance of Business Growth
    b. Overview of the Book's Structure
2. **Chapter 1: Understanding Your Business Environment**
    a. Market Research and Analysis
    b. Case Study: Market Analysis for a New Product Launch
3. **Chapter 2: Crafting a Winning Business Strategy**
    a. Vision and Mission Statements
    b. SWOT Analysis
    c. Case Study: Strategic Planning for a Tech Startup
4. **Chapter 3: Digital Marketing Mastery**
    a. Social Media Marketing
    b. SEO and Content Marketing
    c. Email Marketing

d. Case Study: Social Media Campaign for an E-commerce Brand
5. **Chapter 4: Financial Management**
   a. Budgeting and Financial Planning
   b. Investment Strategies
   c. Case Study: Financial Turnaround for a Small Business
6. **Chapter 5: Leadership and Team Building**
   a. Leadership Styles
   b. Building and Managing Teams
   c. Case Study: Team Building in a Growing Company
7. **Chapter 6: Customer Relationship Management**
   a. Customer Retention Strategies
   b. Building Customer Loyalty
   c. Case Study: CRM Implementation in a Service Industry
8. **Chapter 7: Innovation and Adaptability**
   a. Fostering Innovation in Your Business
   b. Adapting to Market Changes
   c. Case Study: Innovation in a Traditional Industry
9. **Chapter 8: Operational Excellence**
   a. Streamlining Processes
   b. Quality Management

      c. Case Study: Operational Improvements in a Manufacturing Business

10. **Chapter 9: Sales and Marketing Alignment**
    a. Integrating Sales and Marketing Efforts
    b. Measuring Success
    c. Case Study: Sales and Marketing Integration in a Retail Business

11. **Chapter 10: Scaling Your Business**
    a. Strategies for Growth
    b. Managing Growing Pains
    c. Case Study: Scaling a Tech Company

12. **Conclusion**
    a. Recap of Key Strategies
    b. Encouragement for Implementation
    c. Final Thoughts

CHAPTER 1: UNDERSTANDING YOUR BUSINESS Environment

A deep understanding of your business environment is essential for making informed decisions, identifying opportunities, and mitigating risks. This chapter will cover the importance of market research and analysis, and present a case study on market analysis for a new product launch.

MARKET RESEARCH AND ANALYSIS

Market research involves gathering, analyzing, and interpreting information about a market, including information about the target market, consumers, competitors, and the industry as a whole. It's a crucial step in understanding the business environment and making strategic decisions.

KEY COMPONENTS OF MARKET RESEARCH

1. Defining the Objective: Clearly define what you aim to achieve with your market research. This could be understanding customer needs, evaluating market demand, or identifying potential competitors.

2. Research Design: Choose the methods you'll use to gather data. This can include surveys, interviews, focus groups, and secondary research from existing sources.

3. Data Collection: Gather the data using the chosen methods. Ensure that the data is accurate and representative of the target market.

4. Data Analysis: Analyze the collected

data to extract meaningful insights. Use statistical tools and software to identify trends, patterns, and correlations.
5. Reporting and Interpretation: Present the findings in a clear and actionable manner. Provide recommendations based on the insights gained from the analysis.

MARKET ANALYSIS

Market analysis is a detailed assessment of a market within a specific industry. It involves evaluating the market size, growth rate, trends, competition, and potential opportunities.

1. Market Size and Growth: Determine the current size of the market and its growth potential. Use historical data and growth projections to assess future trends.

2. Market Segmentation: Segment the market into distinct groups based on demographics, psychographics, geographic location, and behavior. This helps in targeting specific segments more effectively.

3. Competitive Analysis: Identify key competitors and evaluate their strengths and weaknesses. Analyze their market positioning, pricing strategies, and unique selling propositions (USPs).

4. SWOT Analysis: Conduct a SWOT analysis to identify the strengths, weaknesses, opportunities, and threats related to your business and the market environment.
5. Consumer Behavior: Understand the buying behavior of your target customers. Analyze factors such as purchasing patterns, preferences, and decision-making processes.

CASE STUDY: MARKET ANALYSIS FOR A NEW PRODUCT LAUNCH

Background: Rockon Foods, a company specializing in organic snacks, planned to launch a new line of healthy energy bars. To ensure a successful launch, they conducted comprehensive market research and analysis.

Objective: The primary objective was to understand the demand for healthy energy bars, identify the target market, and evaluate the competitive landscape.

RESEARCH DESIGN AND DATA COLLECTION:

- Surveys: Conducted online surveys targeting health-conscious consumers to understand their preferences and buying behavior.
- Focus Groups: Organized focus group discussions to gather qualitative insights on taste preferences and packaging designs.
- Secondary Research: Analyzed industry reports, market trends, and competitor data from existing sources.

DATA ANALYSIS:

- Market Size and Growth: The analysis revealed that the healthy snack market was growing at a compound annual growth rate (CAGR) of 8%. The energy bar segment was a significant contributor to this growth.
- Market Segmentation: Identified three primary segments: fitness enthusiasts, busy professionals, and parents looking for healthy snacks for their children.
- Competitive Analysis: Evaluated key competitors like Zilto Snacks and Health Bars Co. Found that competitors focused heavily on protein content but lacked options with diverse flavors.
- SWOT Analysis: Strengths included ABC Foods' strong brand reputation and existing customer base. Weaknesses were limited distribution channels.

Opportunities involved expanding into online sales. Threats included potential entry of new competitors.

- Consumer Behavior: The data showed that taste and nutritional value were the most important factors for consumers when choosing energy bars. Packaging convenience was also a significant consideration.

REPORTING AND INTERPRETATION:

- Based on the analysis, Rockon Foods decided to launch three flavors of energy bars, each targeting a different market segment. They also planned to emphasize the organic ingredients and health benefits in their marketing campaigns.
- Recommendations included investing in online sales platforms and exploring partnerships with gyms and health stores for distribution.

RESULTS:

- The new product line was successfully launched and received positive feedback from the target market. Within six months, sales exceeded projections by 20%, and the company expanded its distribution network.

CONCLUSION

Understanding your business environment through market research and analysis is crucial for making informed strategic decisions. By gathering and analyzing relevant data, you can identify opportunities, mitigate risks, and achieve your business goals more effectively. The case study of ABC Foods illustrates how thorough market analysis can lead to a successful product launch and business growth.

CHAPTER 2: CRAFTING A WINNING BUSINESS STRATEGY

Crafting a winning business strategy requires a clear vision and mission, coupled with a realistic assessment of your strengths, weaknesses, opportunities, and threats (SWOT analysis).

VISION AND MISSION STATEMENTS

Your vision statement defines the long-term goals and aspirations of your business, while your mission statement outlines the purpose and primary objectives.

SWOT ANALYSIS

Conducting a SWOT analysis helps you identify your internal strengths and weaknesses, as well as external opportunities and threats. This strategic planning tool provides a clear picture of where your business stands and what steps you need to take to achieve your goals.

CASE STUDY: STRATEGIC PLANNING FOR A TECH STARTUP

Cee Tech Innovators, a startup in the software development industry, used SWOT analysis to shape their business strategy. They identified their strengths in innovative technology and a skilled team, but also recognized weaknesses in market presence and funding. Opportunities in emerging markets and threats from established competitors were also noted. This analysis guided their strategy to focus on niche markets and secure venture capital, leading to rapid growth and market penetration.

CHAPTER 3: DIGITAL MARKETING MASTERY

In the digital age, marketing has evolved significantly. Leveraging digital platforms to reach and engage with your audience is no longer optional; it's a necessity. This chapter will dive into the essential components of digital marketing, including social media marketing, SEO and content marketing, and email marketing. We will also explore a case study of a successful social media campaign for an e-commerce brand to illustrate these concepts in action.

SOCIAL MEDIA MARKETING

Social media platforms have become powerful tools for businesses to connect with their audience, build brand awareness, and drive sales. Here are key strategies to master social media marketing:

1. **Identify Your Audience**: Understanding your target audience is crucial. Use demographic data, interests, and behaviour analysis to tailor your content to their preferences.

2. **Choose the Right Platforms**: Not all social media platforms will suit your business. Choose platforms where your audience is most active. For instance, Instagram and Pinterest are ideal for visually appealing products, while LinkedIn is great for B2B marketing.

3. **Create Engaging Content**: High-quality, engaging content is the heart of social media marketing. Use a mix of images, videos, stories, and live sessions to keep your audience engaged.

4. **Consistency is Key**: Regular posting and

engagement help build a loyal following. Use social media scheduling tools like Buffer or Hootsuite to maintain a consistent presence.

5. **Analyse and Adjust**: Use analytics tools to track the performance of your posts and campaigns. Adjust your strategy based on what works best.

SEO AND CONTENT MARKETING

Search Engine Optimization (SEO) and content marketing go hand in hand. SEO ensures that your content is discoverable, while content marketing provides value to your audience.

1. **Keyword Research**: Use tools like Google Keyword Planner, SEMrush, or Ahrefs to find relevant keywords that your audience is searching for.
2. **Quality Content**: Create valuable, informative, and engaging content that addresses your audience's needs and interests. Blog posts, articles, videos, and infographics are great formats.
3. **On-Page SEO**: Optimize your content for search engines by using appropriate keywords, meta tags, headers, and alt text for images.
4. **Backlink Building**: Gain high-quality backlinks from reputable sites to boost your search engine ranking. Guest blogging and partnerships can help in this regard.

5. **Regular Updates**: Keep your content fresh and updated to maintain relevance and authority in your industry.

EMAIL MARKETING

Email marketing remains one of the most effective ways to nurture leads and drive sales. Here are strategies to maximize its impact:

1. **Build a Quality Email List**: Use opt-in forms on your website, social media, and during events to grow your email list.
2. **Personalized Content**: Segment your email list based on user behavior, preferences, and demographics to send personalized and relevant content.
3. **Compelling Subject Lines**: Craft attention-grabbing subject lines to improve open rates.
4. **Clear Call-to-Actions (CTAs)**: Ensure your emails have clear and compelling CTAs to drive conversions.
5. **A/B Testing**: Test different versions of your emails to see which ones perform better and refine your strategy accordingly.
6. **Analytics**: Use email marketing tools like Mailchimp, Constant Contact, or Sensible to track the performance of your campaigns and make data-driven decisions.

Case Study: Social Media Campaign for an E-commerce Brand

Background: Rangoon E-commerce, a brand specializing in handmade jewellery, wanted to increase its online presence and drive sales through social media.

Strategy:

1. **Audience Research**: They identified their target audience as women aged 18-35 who are interested in fashion, handmade crafts, and sustainable products.

2. **Platform Selection**: Instagram and Pinterest were chosen as the primary platforms due to their visual nature and popularity among the target demographic.

3. **Content Creation**: High-quality images and videos showcasing the jewellery, behind-the-scenes content of the making process, and customer testimonials were created. They also used Instagram Stories and IGTV to engage their audience.

4. **Influencer Partnerships**: They collaborated with fashion influencers to reach a wider audience and gain credibility.

5. **Consistent Posting**: A content calendar was used to maintain a consistent posting schedule.

6. **Engagement**: They actively engaged with their

audience by responding to comments, hosting giveaways, and running Q&A sessions.

Results:

- **Increased Followers**: Their Instagram followers grew by 50% within three months.
- **Higher Engagement**: Engagement rates on their posts increased by 35%.
- **Sales Boost**: Online sales increased by 40% during the campaign period.
- **Brand Awareness**: The collaboration with influencers significantly boosted brand visibility and credibility.

This case study illustrates the power of a well-planned and executed social media campaign in driving business growth. By understanding and implementing these digital marketing strategies, you can effectively reach your target audience, build a strong online presence, and achieve your business goals.

CHAPTER 4: FINANCIAL MANAGEMENT

Effective financial management is the cornerstone of any successful business. It involves budgeting, financial planning, and making smart investment decisions to ensure long-term profitability and sustainability. In this chapter, we will explore key strategies for financial management, including budgeting and financial planning, investment strategies, and a case study on the financial turnaround of a small business.

Budgeting and Financial Planning

Budgeting and financial planning are critical for managing your business's finances effectively. Here's how you can create a robust financial plan:

1. **Set Clear Financial Goals**: Define short-term and long-term financial objectives. This could include targets for revenue, profit margins, cost reduction, and expansion.

2. **Create a Detailed Budget**: Develop a comprehensive budget that outlines your

expected income and expenses. Include categories such as operational costs, salaries, marketing, and contingencies.

3. **Monitor Cash Flow**: Keep track of your cash inflows and outflows to ensure you have enough liquidity to cover your expenses. Use cash flow statements to analyze your financial health regularly.

4. **Adjust and Adapt**: Review your budget periodically and adjust it based on actual performance and changing market conditions. Flexibility is key to effective financial planning.

5. **Use Financial Software**: Tools like QuickBooks, Xero, or FreshBooks can help automate your financial management processes, making it easier to track and manage your finances.

Investment Strategies

Investing wisely is crucial for business growth and financial stability. Here are some investment strategies to consider:

1. **Diversify Investments**: Spread your investments across different asset classes to reduce risk. This could include stocks, bonds, real estate, and mutual funds.

2. **Reinvest Profits**: Allocate a portion of your profits back into the business to fund growth initiatives, such as new

product development, marketing campaigns, or technology upgrades.

3. **Evaluate Risks**: Assess the risks associated with each investment opportunity. Consider factors such as market volatility, potential returns, and your risk tolerance.
4. **Seek Professional Advice**: Consult with financial advisors or investment experts to make informed decisions. They can provide valuable insights and help you develop a tailored investment strategy.
5. **Monitor Performance**: Regularly review the performance of your investments and make adjustments as needed to align with your financial goals.

Case Study: Financial Turnaround for a Small Business

Background: Rexwell Bakery, a small family-owned business, was struggling with declining sales, high operating costs, and mounting debt. The owners decided to implement a comprehensive financial management strategy to turn the business around.

Strategy:

1. **Budgeting and Cost Control**: They created a detailed budget to monitor expenses closely. By negotiating better deals with suppliers and reducing waste, they were able to cut costs by 20%.

2. **Cash Flow Management**: They improved cash flow by offering early payment discounts to customers and extending payment terms with suppliers. This helped them maintain a positive cash balance.

3. **Revenue Enhancement**: They introduced new product lines and leveraged social media marketing to attract more customers. This resulted in a 30% increase in sales within six months.

4. **Debt Restructuring**: They worked with their bank to restructure their debt, securing lower interest rates and extended repayment terms. This reduced their monthly debt payments by 15%.

5. **Investment in Technology**: They invested in a point-of-sale (POS) system to streamline operations and track sales data more efficiently. This improved inventory management and reduced stockouts.

Results:

- **Increased Profitability**: The bakery's profit margins improved from 5% to 15% within a year.
- **Enhanced Cash Flow**: Better cash flow management allowed them to pay off debt faster and reinvest in the business.
- **Sustainable Growth**: The new product lines

and marketing strategies attracted a loyal customer base, ensuring steady revenue growth.

This case study demonstrates how effective financial management can lead to a successful business turnaround. By setting clear financial goals, implementing sound budgeting practices, and making strategic investments, businesses can achieve financial stability and growth.

In conclusion, mastering financial management is essential for any business aiming to thrive in a competitive environment. By following the strategies outlined in this chapter, you can build a solid financial foundation, make informed investment decisions, and navigate your business towards long-term success.

CHAPTER 5: LEADERSHIP AND TEAM BUILDING

Effective leadership and strong team building are fundamental to any business's success. They drive motivation, foster innovation, and create a cohesive work environment. This chapter explores various leadership styles, strategies for building and managing teams, and presents a case study on team building in a growing company.

Leadership Styles

Understanding and adopting the right leadership style can significantly impact your team's performance and morale. Here are some common leadership styles:

1. **Autocratic Leadership**: Involves making decisions unilaterally without much input from team members. Effective in situations requiring quick decision-making but can demotivate team members if overused.

2. **Democratic Leadership**: Encourages team participation in decision-making. This style

fosters collaboration and creativity but can be time-consuming.

3. **Transformational Leadership**: Focuses on inspiring and motivating team members to exceed expectations and embrace change. Ideal for driving innovation and long-term growth.

4. **Transactional Leadership**: Based on a system of rewards and punishments. Useful for achieving short-term goals but may not foster long-term loyalty and engagement.

5. **Servant Leadership**: Prioritizes the needs of team members, empowering them to perform at their best. This style builds strong relationships and a supportive work environment.

Building and Managing Teams

Creating and managing a high-performing team requires strategic planning and ongoing effort. Here are key strategies for effective team building and management:

1. **Define Roles and Responsibilities**: Clearly outline each team member's roles and responsibilities to avoid confusion and ensure accountability.

2. **Foster Open Communication**: Encourage transparent and open communication within the team. This helps in building trust and addressing issues promptly.

3. **Encourage Collaboration**: Promote a culture of collaboration where team members are encouraged to share ideas and work together towards common goals.
4. **Provide Training and Development**: Invest in the continuous development of your team through training programs, workshops, and mentoring.
5. **Recognize and Reward Achievements**: Acknowledge and reward the contributions and achievements of team members to boost morale and motivation.
6. **Build a Positive Work Environment**: Create a work environment that is supportive, inclusive, and conducive to productivity.

Case Study: Team Building in a Growing Company

Background: Natural Tech, a mid-sized technology company, experienced rapid growth over two years. With this growth, the company faced challenges in maintaining team cohesion and managing new hires effectively.

Strategy:

1. **Leadership Training**: The company invested in leadership development programs for managers to equip them with the skills needed to lead larger, more diverse teams.

2. **Onboarding Program**: They implemented a comprehensive onboarding program to integrate new hires smoothly and align them with the company's culture and values.

3. **Team Building Activities**: Regular team-building activities, such as workshops, retreats, and social events, were organized to strengthen relationships and foster a sense of belonging.

4. **Mentorship Program**: Senior employees were paired with new hires in a mentorship program to provide guidance, support, and knowledge transfer.

5. **Feedback Mechanisms**: The company established regular feedback sessions and anonymous surveys to gauge employee satisfaction and address concerns.

Results:

- **Improved Employee Retention**: The turnover rate decreased by 20% as employees felt more connected and valued.

- **Enhanced Team Cohesion**: Team members reported stronger relationships and improved collaboration, leading to higher productivity.

- **Positive Work Culture**: The company's culture became more inclusive and supportive, attracting top talent in the industry.

This case study highlights how strategic

team building and leadership development can address the challenges of a growing company. By investing in their leaders and fostering a supportive work environment, Natural Tech was able to maintain team cohesion and drive continued success.

In conclusion, effective leadership and team building are crucial for any business aiming to achieve sustainable growth and success. By understanding different leadership styles, implementing strategic team-building practices, and learning from real-world examples, you can create a high-performing team that drives your business forward.

CHAPTER 6: CUSTOMER RELATIONSHIP MANAGEMENT

Customer Relationship Management (CRM) is a critical aspect of any business that aims to build lasting relationships with its customers. Effective CRM strategies can lead to increased customer satisfaction, higher retention rates, and enhanced customer loyalty. This chapter will explore customer retention strategies, methods to build customer loyalty, and provide a case study on CRM implementation in the service industry.

Customer Retention Strategies

Retaining existing customers is more cost-effective than acquiring new ones. Here are some strategies to enhance customer retention:

1. **Personalized Communication**: Tailor your communication to meet the individual needs and preferences of your customers. Use CRM tools to track customer interactions and

personalize emails, offers, and services.

2. **Customer Feedback**: Regularly solicit feedback from your customers to understand their needs and expectations. Use this feedback to improve your products and services.

3. **Loyalty Programs**: Implement loyalty programs that reward customers for their continued patronage. Offer discounts, exclusive deals, or points that can be redeemed for future purchases.

4. **Proactive Support**: Anticipate customer issues and address them proactively. Provide excellent customer service and ensure that any problems are resolved quickly and efficiently.

5. **Consistent Engagement**: Maintain regular contact with your customers through newsletters, social media, and other channels. Keep them informed about new products, services, and updates.

6. **Quality Assurance**: Ensure that your products and services consistently meet high standards of quality. Satisfied customers are more likely to return and recommend your business to others.

Building Customer Loyalty

Customer loyalty is built over time through positive experiences and trust. Here are some ways to foster customer loyalty:

1. **Deliver Exceptional Service**: Provide outstanding customer service at every touchpoint. Train your staff to be courteous, knowledgeable, and responsive to customer needs.
2. **Build Trust**: Be transparent and honest in your dealings with customers. Keep your promises and handle any issues with integrity.
3. **Create Value**: Offer products and services that provide real value to your customers. Continuously innovate and improve to meet their evolving needs.
4. **Engage on Social Media**: Use social media platforms to engage with your customers, answer their questions, and build a community around your brand.
5. **Show Appreciation**: Regularly show your appreciation for your customers. Send thank-you notes, offer special discounts, or recognize them on social media.
6. **Personal Connections**: Develop personal connections with your customers. Remember important details about them and their preferences, and use this information to make their experiences more enjoyable.

Case Study: CRM Implementation in a Service Industry

Background: Zoobie Spa, a mid-sized wellness and spa center, faced challenges in managing customer interactions and improving customer satisfaction. They decided to implement a CRM system to streamline their processes and enhance customer relationships.

Strategy:

1. **CRM Software Selection**: Zoobie Spa chose a CRM software that offered features such as appointment scheduling, customer feedback management, and personalized marketing.
2. **Staff Training**: The staff was trained on how to use the CRM system effectively. This included managing customer data, scheduling appointments, and tracking customer preferences.
3. **Personalized Services**: Using the CRM system, Zoobie Spa began offering personalized services based on customer preferences and history. Customers received tailored recommendations for treatments and products.
4. **Feedback Integration**: Customer feedback was collected through the CRM system and used to make improvements. This helped Zoobie Spa to address issues quickly and enhance the customer experience.
5. **Loyalty Program**: A loyalty program was integrated into the CRM system, allowing customers to earn points for every visit and

redeem them for discounts or free services.

Results:

- **Increased Customer Satisfaction:** Customer satisfaction scores increased by 25% due to personalized services and proactive support.
- **Higher Retention Rates:** The retention rate improved by 30% as customers appreciated the tailored experiences and loyalty rewards.
- **Operational Efficiency:** The CRM system streamlined operations, reducing appointment scheduling errors and improving staff productivity.

This case study illustrates how implementing a CRM system can significantly improve customer relationships and drive business success. By leveraging CRM tools and strategies, Zoobie Spa was able to enhance customer satisfaction, boost retention rates, and create a loyal customer base.

In conclusion, effective customer relationship management is essential for building strong, lasting relationships with your customers. By implementing retention strategies, fostering loyalty, and utilizing CRM systems, businesses can improve customer satisfaction and drive long-term success.

CHAPTER 7: INNOVATION AND ADAPTABILITY

Innovation and adaptability are key drivers of business growth and sustainability in today's fast-paced market. Companies that foster a culture of innovation and remain flexible in the face of market changes are better equipped to thrive. This chapter explores strategies to foster innovation in your business, how to adapt to market changes, and provides a case study on innovation in a traditional industry.

Fostering Innovation in Your Business

Innovation doesn't just happen; it requires a supportive environment and proactive efforts. Here are some strategies to encourage innovation within your organization:

1. **Create an Innovation-Friendly Culture**: Foster a culture that values creativity and risk-taking. Encourage employees to share their ideas and support them in exploring new solutions.

2. **Invest in Research and Development**: Allocate

resources to research and development (R&D) to explore new technologies and methodologies. Regularly review and assess R&D projects to ensure alignment with business goals.

3. **Encourage Continuous Learning**: Promote a learning culture where employees are encouraged to acquire new skills and knowledge. Offer training programs, workshops, and opportunities for professional development.

4. **Collaborate and Network**: Engage in partnerships with other businesses, academic institutions, and industry experts. Collaboration can lead to new ideas and innovative solutions.

5. **Empower Employees**: Give employees the autonomy to experiment and take ownership of their projects. Empowered employees are more likely to think creatively and drive innovation.

6. **Implement an Idea Management System**: Use an idea management system to collect, evaluate, and implement innovative ideas from employees. Recognize and reward those who contribute valuable ideas.

7. **Stay Customer-Focused**: Innovation should aim to solve real customer problems. Regularly gather feedback from customers and use it to

guide your innovation efforts.

Adapting to Market Changes

Adaptability is crucial for businesses to stay competitive and respond effectively to market changes. Here's how to build adaptability into your organization:

1. **Monitor Market Trends**: Stay informed about industry trends, emerging technologies, and changes in customer preferences. Use market research and data analysis to anticipate changes.

2. **Flexible Business Models**: Develop flexible business models that can be adjusted quickly in response to market shifts. This includes scalable operations and adaptable supply chains.

3. **Agile Processes**: Implement agile methodologies to enable rapid responses to changes. Agile processes allow for iterative development and continuous improvement.

4. **Diverse Revenue Streams**: Diversify your revenue streams to reduce dependency on a single source of income. This can help mitigate risks associated with market fluctuations.

5. **Responsive Leadership**: Cultivate a leadership team that is proactive and responsive to change. Leaders should be able to make quick decisions and guide the organization through transitions.

6. **Employee Involvement**: Involve employees in the change management process. Communicate transparently about market changes and how they impact the business. Encourage employees to contribute ideas for adaptation.

7. **Continuous Improvement**: Embrace a mindset of continuous improvement. Regularly review business processes and strategies to identify areas for enhancement and adaptation.

Case Study: Innovation in a Traditional Industry

Background: Zeelius Textile, a well-established company in the textile industry, faced declining sales due to increased competition and changing customer preferences. To remain competitive, the company needed to innovate and adapt its traditional business model.

Strategy:

1. **Customer-Centric Innovation**: XYZ Textile conducted extensive market research to understand customer needs and preferences. They identified a growing demand for sustainable and eco-friendly products.

2. **Product Innovation**: The company invested in R&D to develop a new line of sustainable textiles made from organic and recycled materials. They also introduced innovative dyeing techniques that reduced water

consumption and environmental impact.

3. **Digital Transformation**: Zeelius Textile embraced digital transformation by implementing an e-commerce platform and leveraging social media to reach a broader audience. They used data analytics to personalize marketing campaigns and improve customer engagement.

4. **Collaborative Partnerships**: The company partnered with environmental organizations and fashion brands to promote sustainability. These partnerships helped enhance their brand reputation and attract eco-conscious customers.

5. **Agile Manufacturing**: Zeelius Textile adopted agile manufacturing practices to improve efficiency and responsiveness. This allowed them to quickly adapt to changes in demand and reduce lead times.

Results:

- **Increased Sales**: The introduction of sustainable textiles led to a 20% increase in sales within the first year.
- **Enhanced Brand Reputation**: The company's commitment to sustainability attracted positive attention from customers and industry stakeholders, boosting brand reputation.

- **Operational Efficiency**: Agile manufacturing practices improved operational efficiency, reducing production costs by 15%.

This case study demonstrates how innovation and adaptability can transform a traditional industry. By focusing on customer needs, embracing digital tools, and adopting agile practices, Zeelius Textile successfully revitalized its business and achieved significant growth.

In conclusion, fostering innovation and adaptability is essential for business success in a dynamic market. By creating an environment that supports creativity, staying attuned to market changes, and implementing flexible strategies, businesses can thrive and maintain a competitive edge.

CHAPTER 8: OPERATIONAL EXCELLENCE

Operational excellence is crucial for the long-term success and sustainability of any business. It involves streamlining processes, ensuring quality management, and continuously improving operations. This chapter delves into strategies for achieving operational excellence, the importance of quality management, and provides a case study on operational improvements in a manufacturing business.

Streamlining Processes

Streamlining processes involves simplifying and optimizing workflows to improve efficiency, reduce costs, and enhance productivity. Here are some strategies to streamline your business processes:

1. **Process Mapping**: Create detailed maps of your current processes to identify bottlenecks, redundancies, and areas for improvement. Tools like flowcharts and process diagrams can be helpful.

2. **Automation**: Implement automation tools and technologies to handle repetitive tasks. Automation can significantly reduce manual effort, minimize errors, and speed up processes.

3. **Lean Management**: Adopt lean management principles to eliminate waste, improve workflow, and enhance value for customers. Focus on continuous improvement and maximizing efficiency.

4. **Standardization**: Standardize processes to ensure consistency and reliability. Develop standard operating procedures (SOPs) and train employees to follow them.

5. **Data-Driven Decisions**: Use data analytics to monitor process performance and make informed decisions. Track key performance indicators (KPIs) to measure efficiency and identify areas for improvement.

6. **Employee Training**: Invest in employee training and development to ensure they have the skills and knowledge to perform their tasks efficiently. Encourage a culture of continuous learning.

7. **Cross-Functional Teams**: Form cross-functional teams to collaborate on process improvement initiatives. Diverse perspectives can lead to innovative solutions and more effective problem-solving.

Quality Management

Quality management ensures that products and services meet or exceed customer expectations. It involves implementing quality control and quality assurance practices throughout the organization. Here are some key aspects of quality management:

1. **Quality Control (QC)**: QC involves inspecting and testing products at various stages of production to identify defects and ensure compliance with quality standards. Implementing QC measures can help prevent defective products from reaching customers.

2. **Quality Assurance (QA)**: QA focuses on preventing defects by improving processes and systems. It involves setting quality standards, conducting audits, and implementing corrective actions to ensure consistent quality.

3. **Total Quality Management (TQM)**: TQM is a holistic approach to quality management that involves all employees in the continuous improvement of processes, products, and services. It emphasizes customer satisfaction and long-term success.

4. **Six Sigma**: Six Sigma is a data-driven methodology for improving quality by eliminating defects and reducing variability in processes. It involves using statistical tools to identify and address root causes of quality

issues.

5. **Continuous Improvement**: Foster a culture of continuous improvement by encouraging employees to identify and address quality issues. Implement feedback mechanisms and reward employees for their contributions to quality improvement.

6. **Supplier Quality Management**: Ensure that suppliers meet your quality standards by conducting audits and establishing clear quality requirements. Collaborate with suppliers to improve their processes and quality.

Case Study: Operational Improvements in a Manufacturing Business

Background: Roana Manufacturing, a mid-sized company in the automotive industry, faced challenges with production inefficiencies, high defect rates, and rising costs. To remain competitive, the company needed to improve its operational processes and enhance quality.

Strategy:

1. **Process Mapping and Analysis**: Roana Manufacturing conducted a thorough analysis of its production processes using process mapping techniques. They identified bottlenecks, redundant steps, and areas of waste.

2. **Lean Manufacturing Implementation:** The company adopted lean manufacturing principles, focusing on eliminating waste and optimizing workflow. They introduced just-in-time (JIT) production to reduce inventory costs and improve efficiency.

3. **Automation and Technology Integration:** Roana Manufacturing invested in automation technologies, such as robotic process automation (RPA) and advanced manufacturing systems. Automation reduced manual labour, minimized errors, and increased production speed.

4. **Quality Management System (QMS):** The company implemented a robust QMS, incorporating QC and QA practices. They set strict quality standards, conducted regular audits, and used Six Sigma methodologies to address quality issues.

5. **Employee Training and Engagement:** Roana Manufacturing provided comprehensive training to employees on lean principles, quality management, and the use of new technologies. They encouraged employee involvement in continuous improvement initiatives.

Results:

- **Improved Efficiency:** Lean manufacturing and automation led to a 30% increase in production efficiency, reducing lead times and operational costs.

- **Enhanced Quality**: The implementation of a QMS and Six Sigma methodologies resulted in a 40% reduction in defect rates, improving product quality and customer satisfaction.

- **Cost Savings**: JIT production and waste reduction initiatives led to significant cost savings, enhancing the company's profitability.

- **Employee Engagement**: Increased employee involvement in process improvement initiatives fostered a culture of innovation and continuous improvement.

This case study demonstrates how operational excellence can transform a manufacturing business. By streamlining processes, implementing quality management practices, and fostering a culture of continuous improvement, Roana Manufacturing achieved significant operational improvements and sustained growth.

In conclusion, operational excellence is essential for business success. By focusing on streamlining processes, ensuring quality, and continuously improving operations, businesses can enhance efficiency, reduce costs, and deliver high-quality products and services.

CHAPTER 9: SALES AND MARKETING ALIGNMENT

Aligning sales and marketing efforts is crucial for driving business growth and improving overall performance. This chapter explores strategies for integrating sales and marketing, the importance of measuring success, and provides a case study on successful sales and marketing integration in a retail business.

Integrating Sales and Marketing Efforts

Integration between sales and marketing teams can lead to better communication, more cohesive strategies, and improved results. Here are some key strategies for achieving alignment:

1. **Shared Goals and Metrics**: Establish common goals and metrics that both sales and marketing teams are accountable for. This creates a unified vision and ensures both teams are working towards the same objectives.

2. **Regular Communication**: Foster regular communication between sales and marketing teams through joint meetings, collaborative planning sessions, and shared platforms. This ensures everyone is on the same page and can address issues promptly.

3. **Collaborative Content Creation**: Involve the sales team in content creation to ensure marketing materials are relevant and address customer pain points. Sales reps can provide valuable insights into customer needs and preferences.

4. **Lead Scoring and Management**: Develop a lead scoring system to prioritize leads based on their likelihood to convert. Both teams should agree on what constitutes a qualified lead and how leads will be handed off from marketing to sales.

5. **Feedback Loops**: Create feedback loops where sales provide feedback on the quality of leads and marketing campaigns. This helps marketing refine their strategies and ensures sales have the tools they need to succeed.

6. **Sales Enablement**: Equip the sales team with the right resources, such as brochures, case studies, and product demos, to effectively engage and convert leads. Marketing should regularly update these materials based on sales feedback.

Measuring Success

To ensure the effectiveness of sales and marketing alignment, it's important to measure success using relevant metrics. Here are some key performance indicators (KPIs) to track:

1. **Lead Conversion Rate**: Measure the percentage of leads that convert into customers. This indicates the effectiveness of both lead generation and sales efforts.

2. **Sales Cycle Length**: Track the average time it takes to convert a lead into a customer. A shorter sales cycle often indicates better alignment and more efficient processes.

3. **Customer Acquisition Cost (CAC)**: Calculate the total cost of acquiring a new customer, including marketing and sales expenses. Lowering CAC while maintaining or increasing sales indicates improved efficiency.

4. **Revenue Growth**: Monitor overall revenue growth to gauge the impact of sales and marketing alignment on business performance.

5. **Lead Quality**: Assess the quality of leads generated by marketing based on sales feedback. High-quality leads are more likely to convert and result in higher revenue.

6. **Customer Retention Rate**: Measure the percentage of customers who continue to do business with you over time. Strong alignment

can lead to better customer experiences and higher retention rates.

Case Study: Sales and Marketing Integration in a Retail Business

Background: Four Square Retail, a mid-sized retail company, faced challenges with misaligned sales and marketing efforts, leading to inefficiencies and missed opportunities. To improve performance, the company embarked on a project to integrate their sales and marketing teams.

Strategy:

1. **Unified Goals and Metrics**: Four Square Retail established shared goals and metrics for both teams, focusing on lead generation, conversion rates, and revenue growth.
2. **Regular Communication**: The company implemented weekly joint meetings and used collaborative tools like Slack and Trello to enhance communication and collaboration.
3. **Content Collaboration**: Marketing worked closely with sales to create content that addressed customer pain points, leading to more effective campaigns and materials.
4. **Lead Management System**: Four Square Retail developed a lead scoring system to prioritize leads and streamline the handoff process between marketing and sales.
5. **Feedback Mechanism**: Sales provided regular

feedback on lead quality and campaign effectiveness, allowing marketing to make data-driven adjustments.

6. **Sales Enablement Resources**: Marketing created and regularly updated sales enablement materials, such as product guides and customer success stories, to support the sales team.

Results:

- **Increased Lead Conversion**: The lead conversion rate improved by 25%, indicating better alignment and more effective lead nurturing.
- **Shorter Sales Cycle**: The sales cycle length decreased by 15%, resulting in faster deal closures and improved efficiency.
- **Reduced CAC**: Customer acquisition costs were reduced by 20%, demonstrating improved cost-effectiveness of marketing and sales efforts.
- **Revenue Growth**: Four Square Retail experienced a 30% increase in revenue within the first year of implementing the integration strategies.
- **Higher Lead Quality**: Sales reported a significant improvement in lead quality, with more leads being ready to purchase and easier

to convert.

This case study highlights the importance of integrating sales and marketing efforts to achieve better business outcomes. By aligning goals, fostering communication, and leveraging feedback, Four Square Retail was able to improve efficiency, increase revenue, and enhance overall performance.

In conclusion, sales and marketing alignment is essential for driving business success. By implementing shared goals, enhancing communication, and measuring success through relevant metrics, businesses can achieve significant improvements in lead conversion, efficiency, and revenue growth.

CHAPTER 10: SCALING YOUR BUSINESS

Scaling a business involves more than just increasing sales and revenue; it requires strategic planning, efficient management, and adaptability to handle new challenges. This chapter delves into effective strategies for growth, managing growing pains, and provides a case study on scaling a tech company.

Strategies for Growth

1. **Market Expansion**: Entering new markets can significantly boost growth. This involves researching potential markets, understanding local regulations, and adapting your product or service to meet local needs.

2. **Product Diversification**: Introducing new products or services can attract new customers and increase sales. This strategy requires market research and innovation to ensure the new offerings meet customer

demands.

3. **Partnerships and Alliances**: Forming strategic partnerships can provide access to new markets, resources, and expertise. Collaborating with other businesses can accelerate growth and create synergies.

4. **Investing in Technology**: Leveraging technology can improve efficiency, reduce costs, and enhance customer experiences. Investing in automation, data analytics, and customer relationship management (CRM) systems can support scaling efforts.

5. **Building a Strong Brand**: A strong brand can differentiate your business from competitors and foster customer loyalty. Consistent branding, effective marketing, and excellent customer service are crucial for building a reputable brand.

6. **Customer Retention**: Focusing on customer retention can be more cost-effective than acquiring new customers. Implementing loyalty programs, providing exceptional service, and engaging with customers can enhance retention rates.

Managing Growing Pains

1. **Maintaining Quality**: As your business grows, maintaining the quality of your products or services is essential. Implementing robust quality control processes and investing in

employee training can help sustain high standards.

2. **Scalable Infrastructure**: Ensure your infrastructure can support growth. This includes having adequate IT systems, physical space, and supply chain capabilities to handle increased demand.

3. **Financial Management**: Effective financial management is crucial during growth. This involves budgeting, forecasting, and securing funding to support expansion efforts.

4. **Human Resources**: Scaling often requires hiring additional staff. Developing a strong recruitment process, providing training, and fostering a positive company culture can attract and retain top talent.

5. **Customer Service**: As your customer base grows, maintaining high levels of customer service can be challenging. Implementing scalable customer service solutions, such as chatbots and self-service options, can help manage increased demand.

Case Study: Scaling a Tech Company

Background: Innovate Tech, a mid-sized tech company, experienced rapid growth due to the success of their innovative software solutions. To scale effectively, they implemented several strategies.

Strategy:

1. **Market Expansion**: Innovate Tech entered new international markets, adapting their software to meet local needs and comply with regulations.

2. **Product Diversification**: They introduced complementary products, such as mobile applications and cloud services, to attract a broader customer base.

3. **Partnerships**: Innovate Tech formed alliances with larger tech companies, gaining access to new markets and resources.

4. **Technology Investment**: They invested in scalable cloud infrastructure and advanced data analytics to improve efficiency and customer insights.

5. **Brand Building**: Innovate Tech launched targeted marketing campaigns and participated in industry events to strengthen their brand and reputation.

Managing Growing Pains:

1. **Quality Control**: They implemented rigorous quality assurance processes to maintain high standards as they scaled.

2. **Scalable Infrastructure**: Innovate Tech upgraded their IT systems and expanded their office space to support growth.

3. **Financial Management**: They secured venture capital funding and developed detailed

financial plans to manage cash flow and investment needs.

4. **HR Expansion**: Innovate Tech hired additional staff, providing comprehensive training programs to ensure new hires were well-prepared.
5. **Customer Service**: They introduced a multi-tiered customer support system, including a knowledge base and live chat options, to handle increased customer inquiries.

Results:

- **Revenue Growth**: Innovate Tech's revenue increased by 50% within two years of implementing their scaling strategies.
- **Market Presence**: They successfully entered three new international markets, expanding their customer base.
- **Product Adoption**: The introduction of new products resulted in a 30% increase in product adoption rates.
- **Customer Satisfaction**: Despite rapid growth, customer satisfaction remained high due to their robust support systems and quality control measures.

CONCLUSION

Recap of Key Strategies

In this book, we explored various strategies to help your business grow and thrive. From mastering digital marketing and financial management to building strong leadership and customer relationships, each chapter provided actionable insights and real-world case studies.

Encouragement for Implementation

Implementing these strategies requires dedication, adaptability, and a willingness to learn and grow. By applying the principles and techniques discussed, you can overcome challenges, seize opportunities, and drive your business towards sustained success.

Final Thoughts

Remember, the journey of business growth is continuous. Stay focused, keep innovating, and always strive for excellence. With the right strategies and a proactive mindset, you can achieve remarkable growth and make a lasting impact in your industry.

AUTHOR: TABREZ NIZAM
@DigitalGrowthExpert

BOOKS BY THIS AUTHOR

Digital Marketing Myths

In the fast-paced world of digital marketing, it's easy to get caught up in the latest trends and buzzwords. But not everything you hear is true. "Digital Marketing Myths" is your guide to separating fact from fiction. This book dives into the most pervasive myths in digital marketing and sets the record straight with evidence-based insights. Whether you're a seasoned marketer or just starting out, this book will help you navigate the digital landscape with confidence and clarity, ensuring you're armed with the right knowledge to make informed decisions. Get ready to debunk myths and elevate your digital marketing game!

www.ingramcontent.com/pod-product-compliance
Lightning Source LLC
Chambersburg PA
CBHW071953210526
45479CB00003B/926

9798333494214